EASY PIANO

SIMPLE CHRISTMAS CAROLS

THE EASIEST EASY PIANO SONGS

ISBN 978-1-5400-2963-8

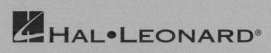

HAL•LEONARD®

Visit Hal Leonard Online at
www.halleonard.com

Contact Us:
Hal Leonard
7777 West Bluemound Road
Milwaukee, WI 53213
Email: info@halleonard.com

In Europe contact:
Hal Leonard Europe Limited
Distribution Centre, Newmarket Road
Bury St Edmunds, Suffolk, IP33 3YB
Email: info@halleonardeurope.com

In Australia contact:
Hal Leonard Australia Pty. Ltd.
4 Lentara Court
Cheltenham, Victoria, 3192 Australia
Email: info@halleonard.com.au

ANGELS WE HAVE HEARD ON HIGH

Traditional French Carol
Translated by JAMES CHADWICK

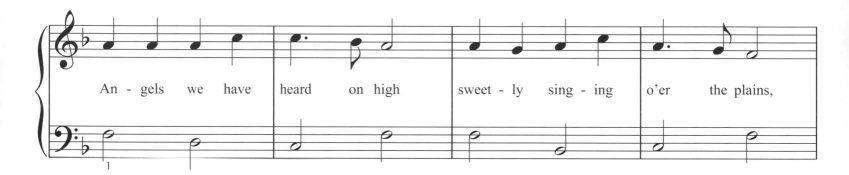

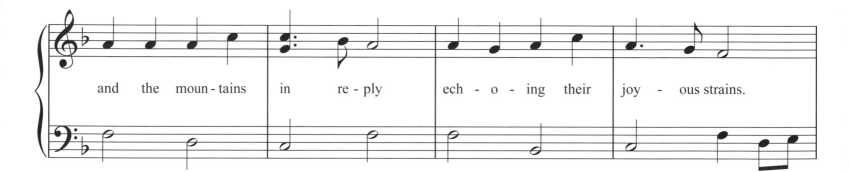

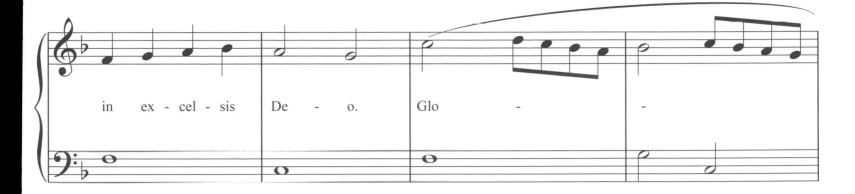

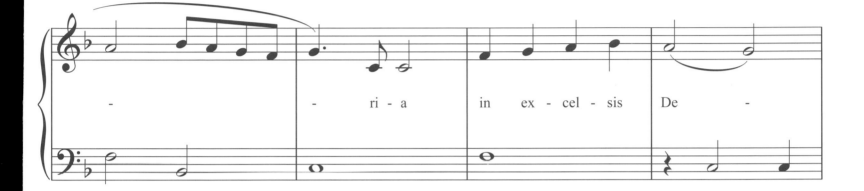

heav'n - ly song? Glo -

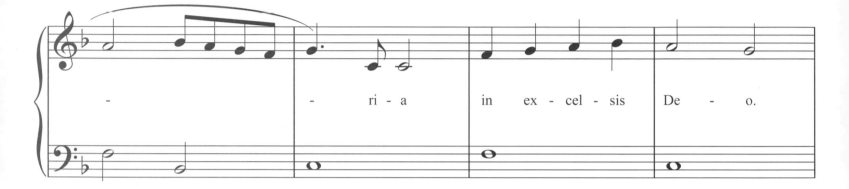

- ri - a in ex - cel - sis De - o.

Glo - - - ri - a

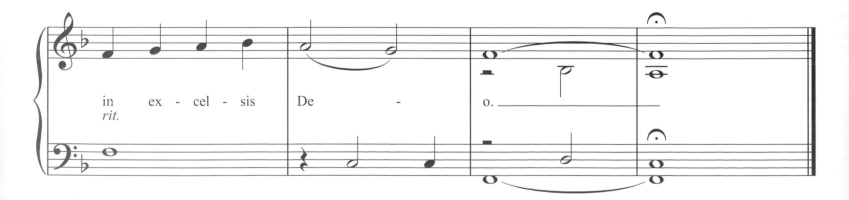

in ex - cel - sis De - o.

rit.

AS WITH GLADNESS MEN OF OLD

Words by WILLIAM CHATTERTON DIX
Music by CONRAD KOCHER

Moderately

As with __ glad - ness
As with __ joy - ful

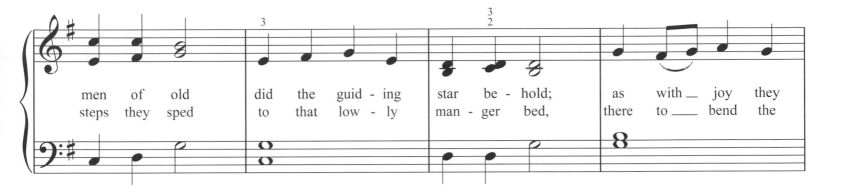

men of old   did the guid - ing   star be - hold;   as with __ joy they
steps they sped   to that low - ly   man - ger bed,   there to __ bend the

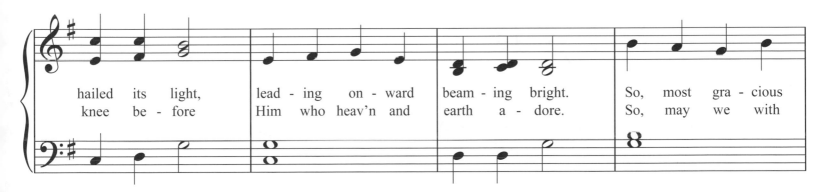

hailed its light,   lead - ing on - ward   beam - ing bright.   So, most gra - cious
knee be - fore   Him who heav'n and   earth a - dore.   So, may we with

Lord, may we   ev - er - more be   led to Thee.
will - ing feet   ev - er seek Thy   mer - cy seat.

AULD LANG SYNE

Words by ROBERT BURNS
Traditional Scottish Melody

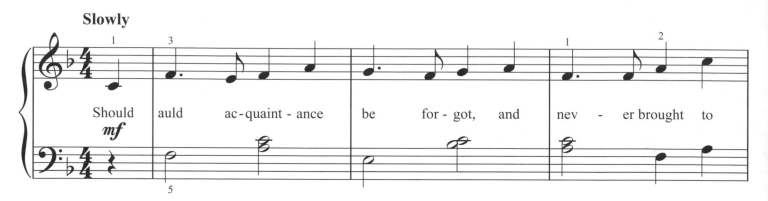

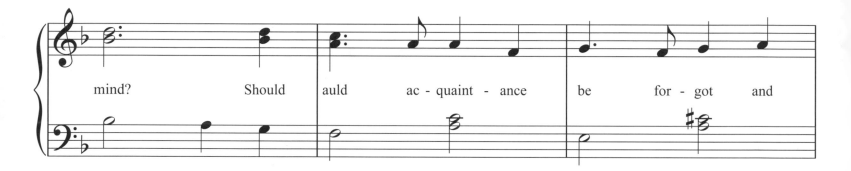

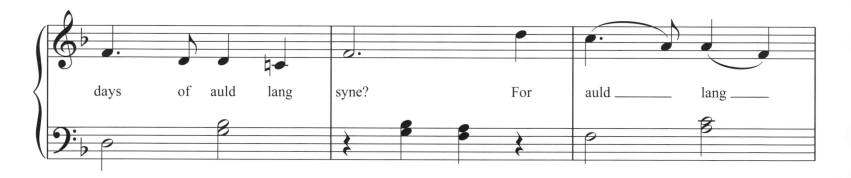

take a cup of kind - ness yet, for _____ auld _____ lang _____

syne. For auld _____ lang _____ syne, my dear, for

auld _____ lang _____ syne, we'll take a cup of

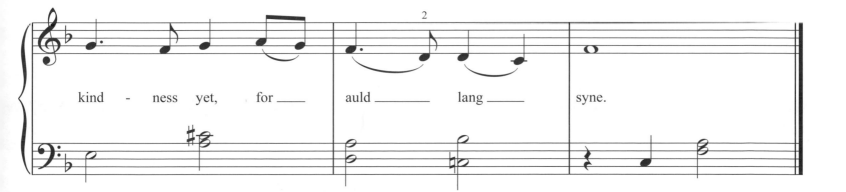

kind - ness yet, for _____ auld _____ lang _____ syne.

AWAY IN A MANGER

Words by JOHN T. McFARLAND (v.3)
Music by JAMES R. MURRAY

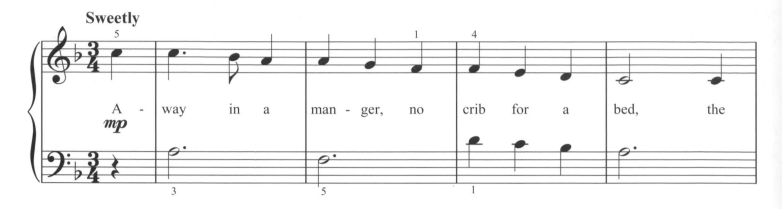

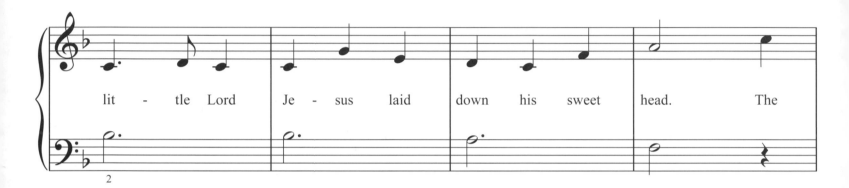

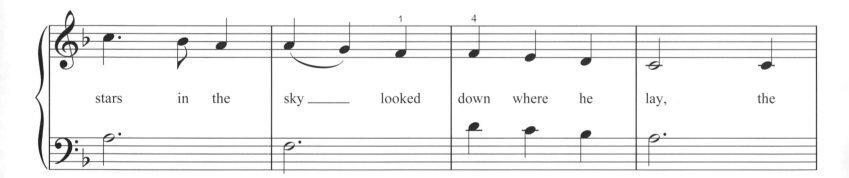

THE BOAR'S HEAD CAROL

Traditional English

With spirit

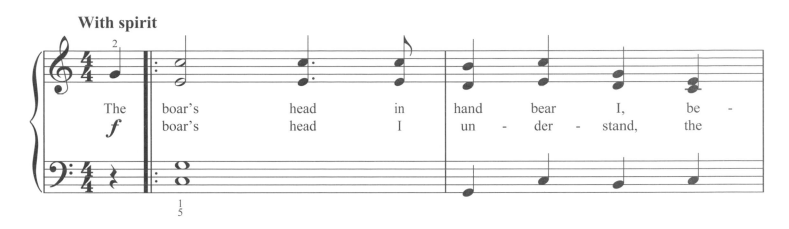

The boar's head in hand bear I, be-
boar's head head I un - der - stand, the

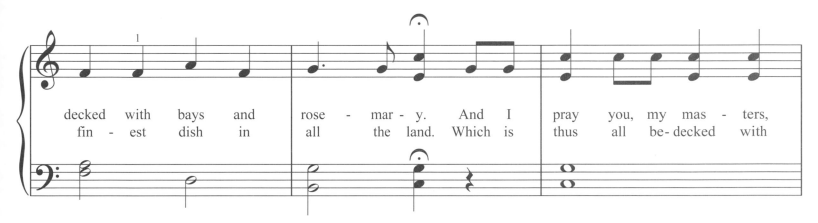

decked with bays and rose - mar - y. And I pray you, my mas - ters,
fin - est dish in all the land. Which is thus all be - decked with

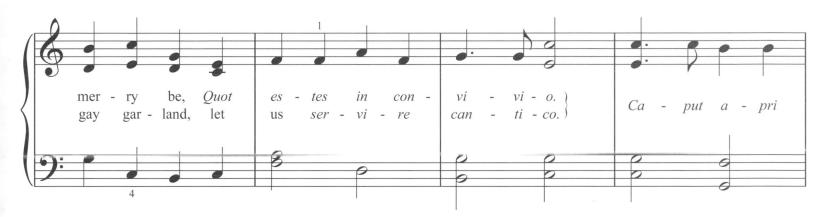

mer - ry be, Quot es - tes in con - vi - vi - o.
gay gar - land, let us ser - vi - re can - ti - co.

Ca - put a - pri

1.
de - fe - ro, red - dens lau - des Do - mi - no. The

2.
Do - mi - no.

BRING A TORCH, JEANNETTE, ISABELLA

17th Century French Provençal Carol

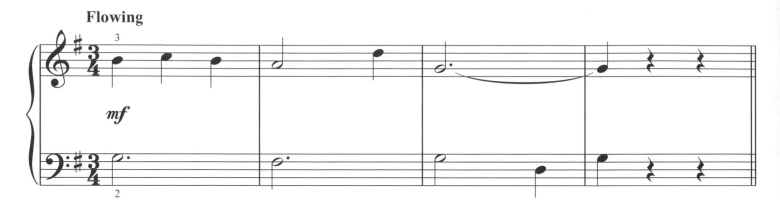

Bring a torch, ____ Jean - nette, Is - a - bel - la,
Has - ten now, ____ good folk of the vil - lage,

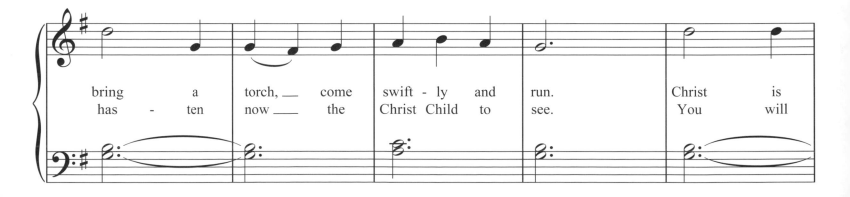

bring a torch, __ come swift - ly and run. Christ is
has - ten now __ the Christ Child to see. You will

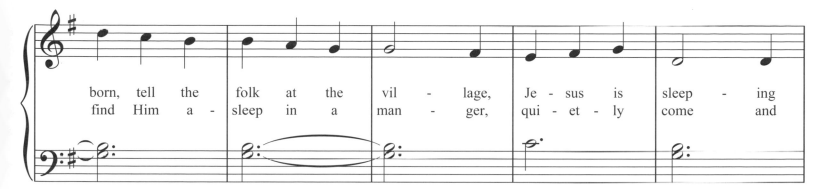

born, tell the folk at the vil - lage, Je - sus is sleep - ing
find Him a - sleep in a man - ger, qui - et - ly come and

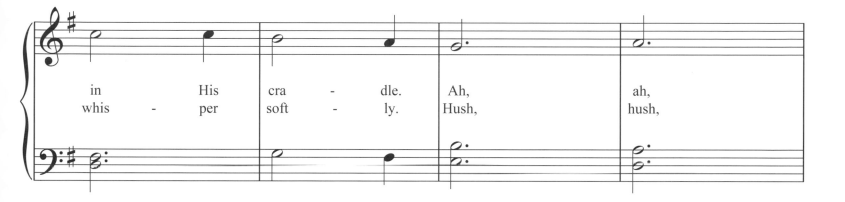

in His cra - dle. Ah,
whis - per soft - ly. Hush,

ah,
hush,

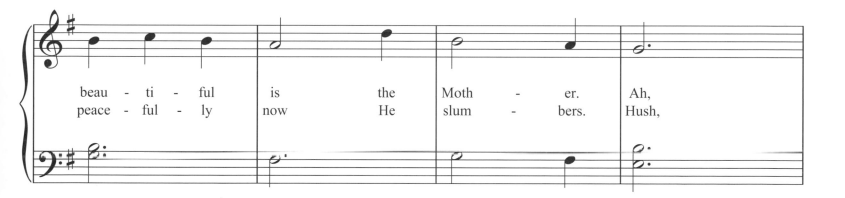

beau - ti - ful is the Moth - er. Ah,
peace - ful - ly now He slum - bers. Hush,

ah, beau - ti - ful is her Son. _____
hush, peace - ful - ly now He sleeps. _____

CAROL OF THE BIRDS

Traditional Catalonian Carol

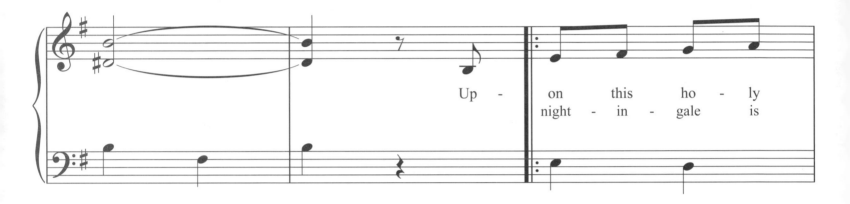

Up - on this ho - ly
night - in - gale is

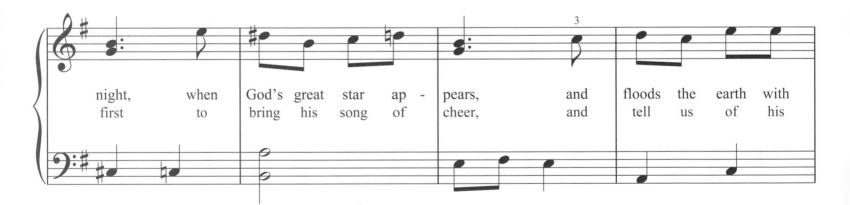

night, when to God's great star ap - pears, and floods the earth with
first to bring his song of cheer, and tell us of his

bright - ness birds' voic - es rise in song, and
glad - ness: Je - sus, our Lord, is born to

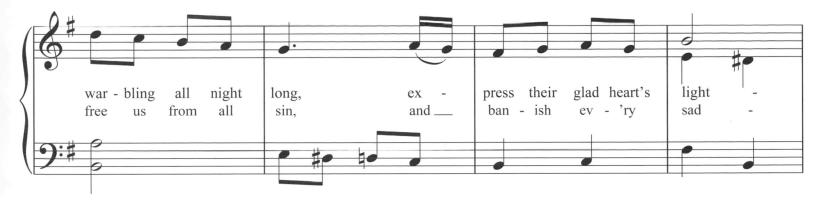

war - bling all night long, ex - press their glad heart's light -
free us from all sin, and ban - ish ev - 'ry sad

ness. Birds' voic - es rise in
ness! Je - sus, our Lord is

song, and, warb - ling all night long, ex -
born to free us from all sin, and

1.
press their glad heart's light - ness. The
ban - ish ev - 'ry sad -

2.
ness.

COME, ALL YE SHEPHERDS

Traditional Czech Text
Traditional Moravian Melody

Happily

Come, all ___ ye ___ shep - herds, ___ such ___ won - ders ___ en - thrall.
Come where ___ the ___ young Child ___ is ___ laid in ___ a ___ stall.

This day to us a Sav - ior is giv - en, whom God on high hath

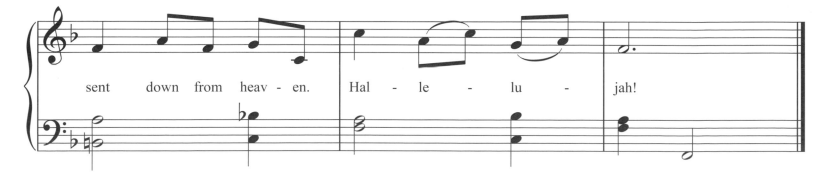

sent down from heav - en. Hal - le - lu - jah!

COVENTRY CAROL

Words by ROBERT CROO
Traditional English Melody

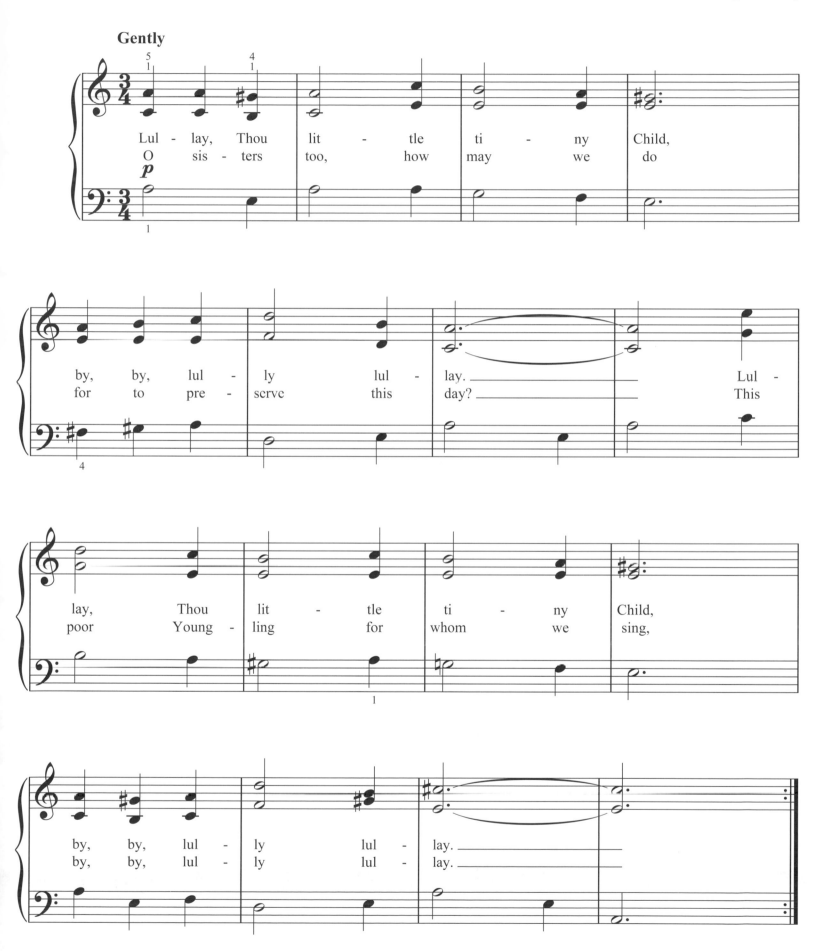

DECK THE HALL

Traditional Welsh Carol

Spirited

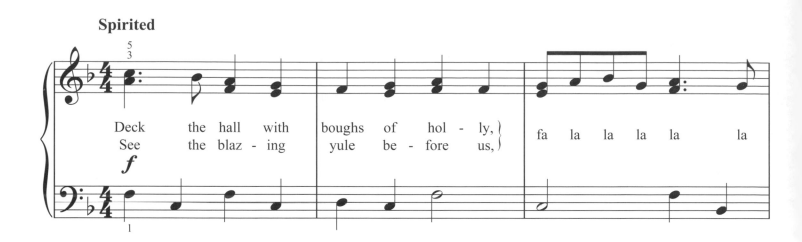

Deck the hall with boughs of hol - ly,
See the blaz - ing yule be - fore us,

fa la la la la la

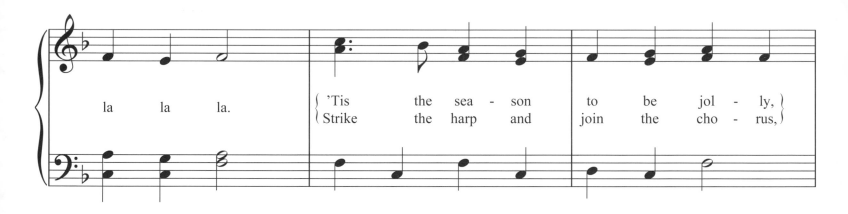

la la la.

'Tis the sea - son to be jol - ly,
Strike the harp and join the cho - rus,

fa la la la la la la la la.

Don we now our
Fol - low me in

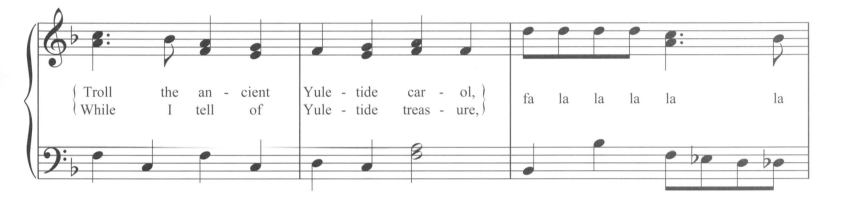

DING DONG! MERRILY ON HIGH!

French Carol

Ding dong! Mer - ri - ly on high the
Ding dong! Car - ol all the bells, ring

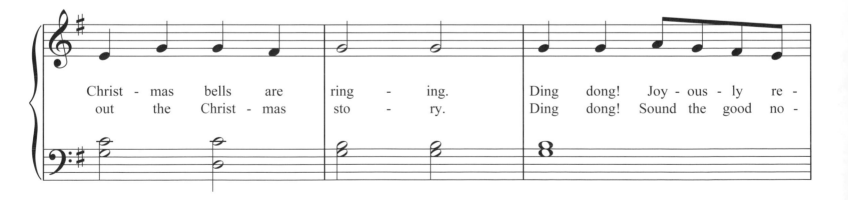

Christ - mas bells are ring - ing. Ding dong! Joy - ous - ly re-
out the Christ - mas sto - ry. Ding dong! Sound the good no-

ply   the an - gels all a - sing - ing.
els,   God's Son has come in glo - ry.

Glo - - -

- - - ri - a, ho -

san - na in ex - cel - sis!   cel - sis!

THE FIRST NOËL

17th Century English Carol
Music from W. Sandys' *Christmas Carols*

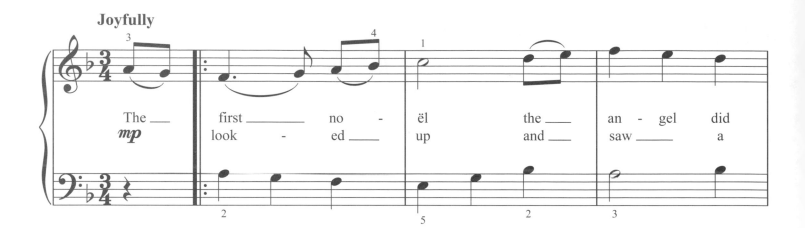

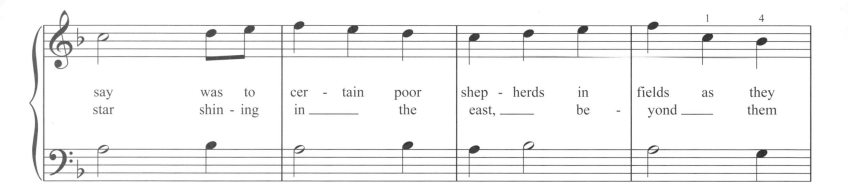

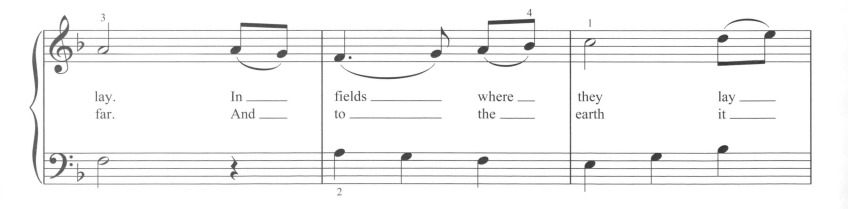

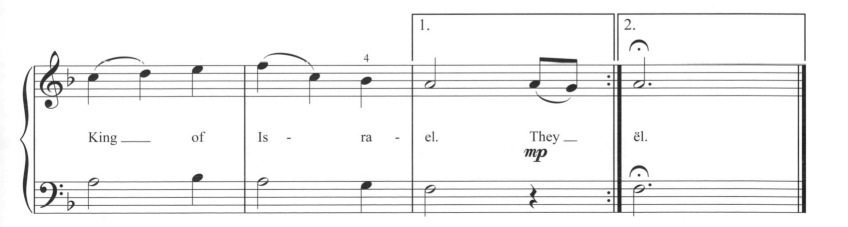

FROM HEAVEN ABOVE
TO EARTH I COME

Words by MARTIN LUTHER
Music from *Geistliche Lieder*, 1539

FUM, FUM, FUM

Traditional Catalonian Carol

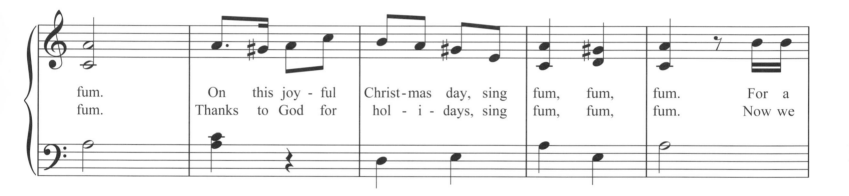

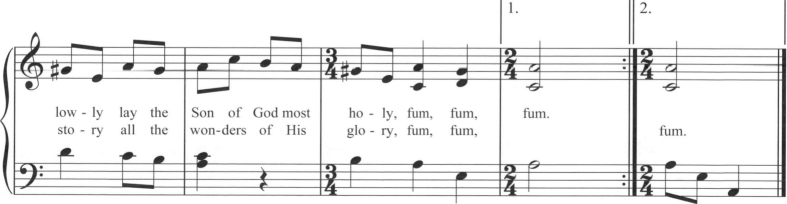

GO, TELL IT ON THE MOUNTAIN

African-American Spiritual
Verses by JOHN W. WORK, JR.

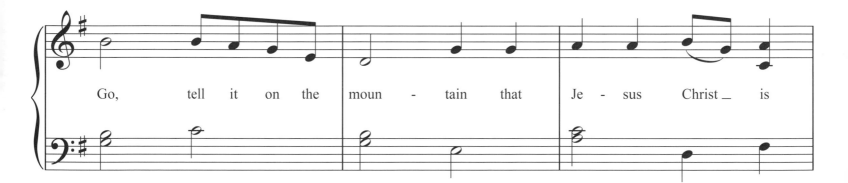

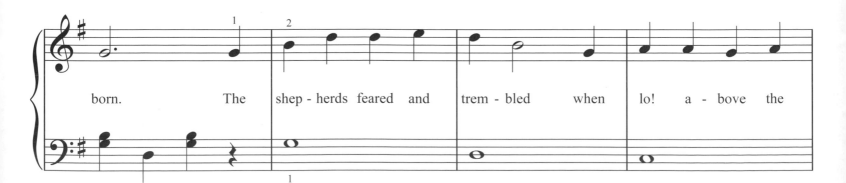

GOD REST YE MERRY, GENTLEMEN

Traditional English Carol

God

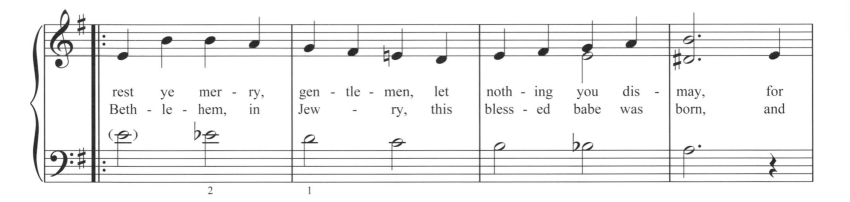

rest ye mer - ry, gen - tle - men, let noth - ing you dis - may, for
Beth - le - hem, in Jew - ry, this bless - ed babe was born, and

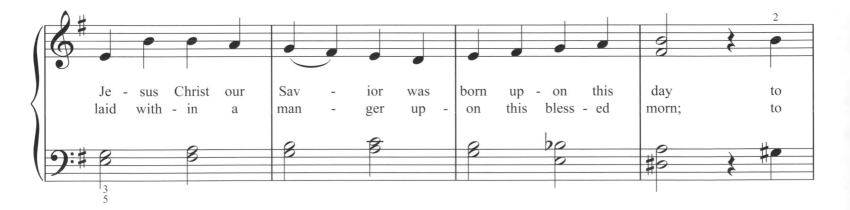

Je - sus Christ our Sav - ior was born up - on this day to
laid with - in a man - ger up - on this bless - ed morn; to

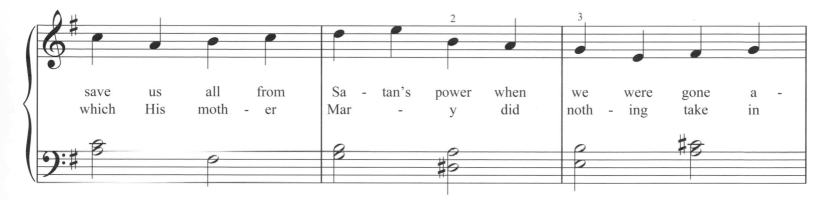

save us all from Sa - tan's power when we were gone a -
which His moth - er Mar - y did noth - ing take in

stray.
scorn. O _____ tid - ings of com - fort and

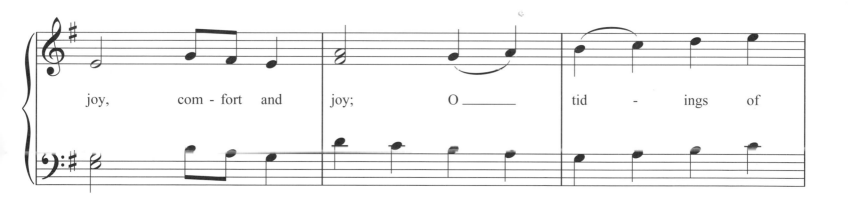

joy, com - fort and joy; O _____ tid - ings of

com - fort and joy! In joy!

29

GOOD CHRISTIAN MEN, REJOICE

14th Century Latin Text
Translated by JOHN MASON NEALE
14th Century German Melody

With spirit

Good Chris - tian men, re - joice _____ with heart and soul and voice, _____

give ye heed to what we say: News! News! Je - sus Christ is

born to - day! Ox and ass be - fore Him bow, and He is in the

man - ger now; Christ is born to - day, _____ Christ is born to -

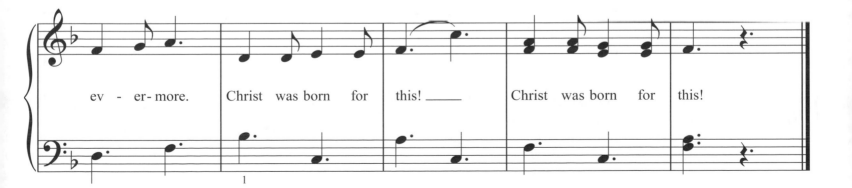

GOOD KING WENCESLAS

Words by JOHN M. NEALE
Music from *Piae Cantiones*

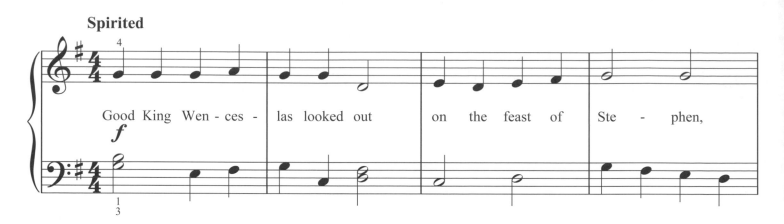

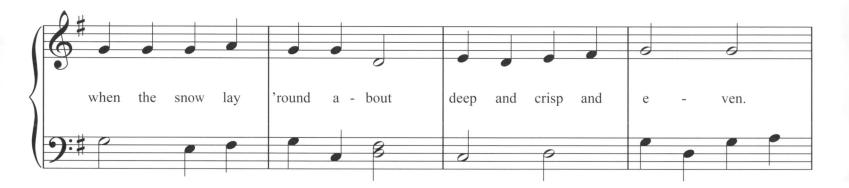

I AM SO GLAD ON CHRISTMAS EVE

Words by MARIE WEXELSEN
Music by PEDER KNUDSEN

Gently

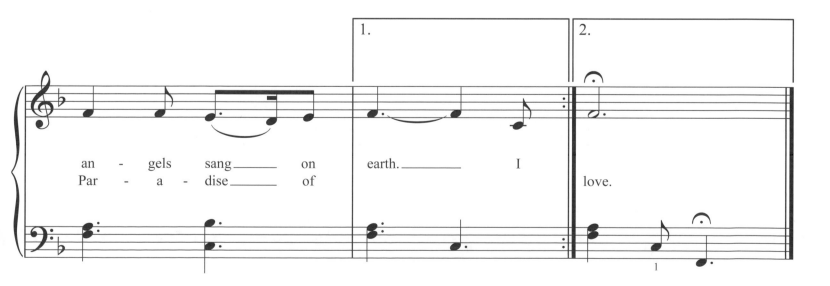

HARK! THE HERALD ANGELS SING

Words by CHARLES WESLEY
Altered by GEORGE WHITEFIELD
Music by FELIX MENDELSSOHN-BARTHOLDY
Arranged by WILLIAM H. CUMMINGS

Moderately

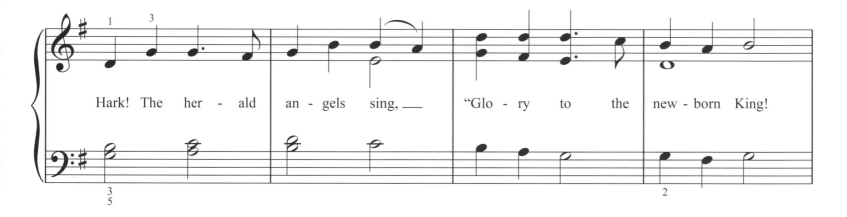

Hark! The her - ald an - gels sing, ___ "Glo - ry to the new - born King!

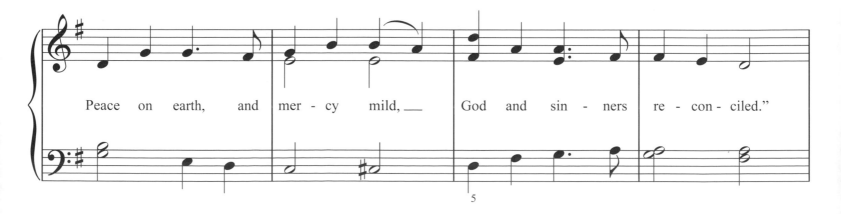

Peace on earth, and mer - cy mild, ___ God and sin - ners re - con - ciled."

Joy - ful all ye na - tions rise, ___ join the tri - umph of the skies. ___

With th'an - gel - ic host pro - claim, "Christ is ___ born in

Beth - le - hem." Hark! The her - ald an - gels sing,

"Glo - ry ___ to the new - born King!"

35

HERE WE COME A-WASSAILING

Traditional

Happily

Here we come a - was - sail - ing a -
We're not dai - ly beg - gars that

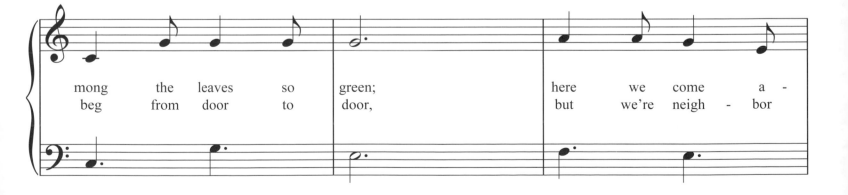

mong the leaves so green;   here we come a -
beg from door to door,   but we're neigh - bor

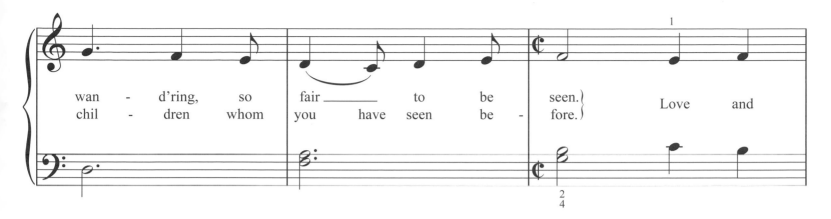

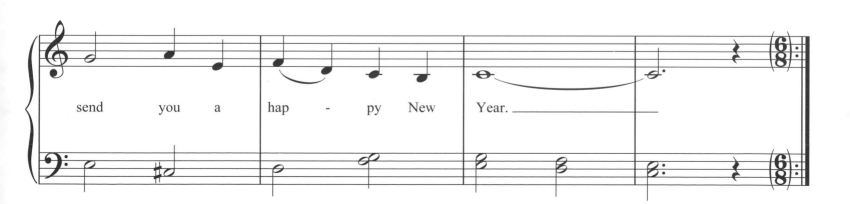

THE HOLLY AND THE IVY

18th Century English Carol

Moderately

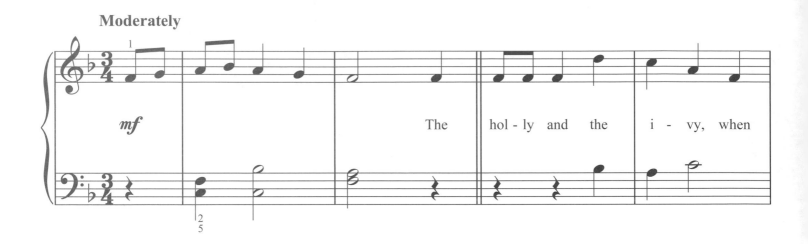

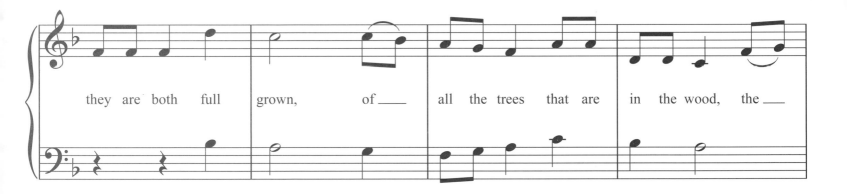

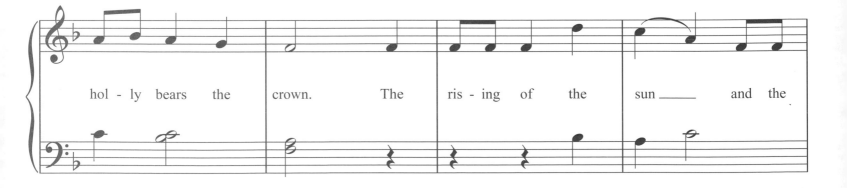

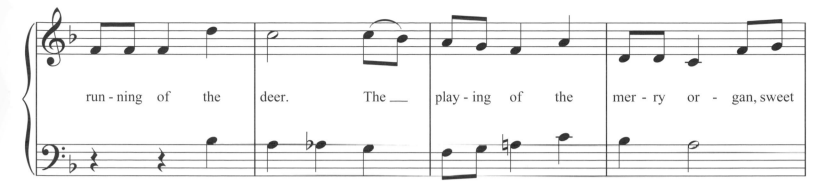

run - ning   of   the   deer.   The ___   play - ing   of   the   mer - ry   or - gan, sweet

sing - ing   in   the   choir.   *cresc.*   The   hol - ly   and   the

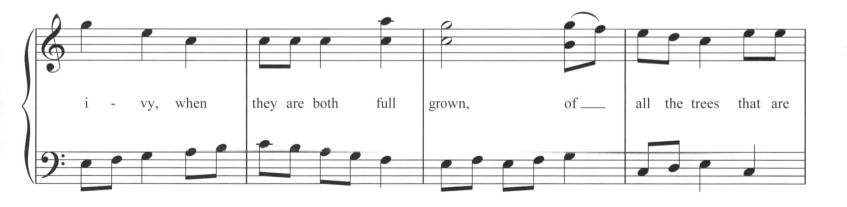

i - vy,   when   they are both   full   grown,   of ___   all   the trees   that are

in   the   wood,   the ___   hol - ly bears the   crown.
rit.

I HEARD THE BELLS ON CHRISTMAS DAY

Words by HENRY WADSWORTH LONGFELLOW
Music by JOHN BAPTISTE CALKIN

Moderately

I
heard the bells on
thought how, as the

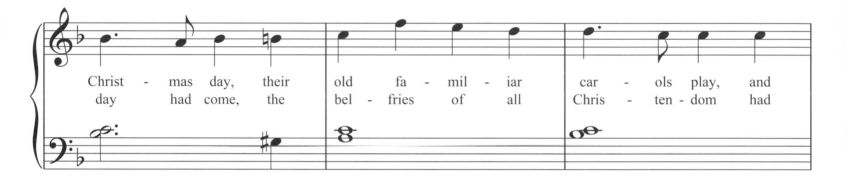

Christ - mas day, their old fa - mil - iar car - ols play, and
day had come, the bel - fries of all Chris - ten - dom had

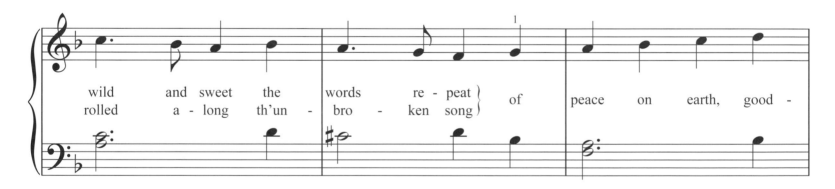

wild and sweet the words re - peat } of peace on earth, good -
rolled a - long th'un - bro - ken song }

1.
will to men.

2.
I will to men.

JINGLE BELLS

Words and Music by
J. PIERPONT

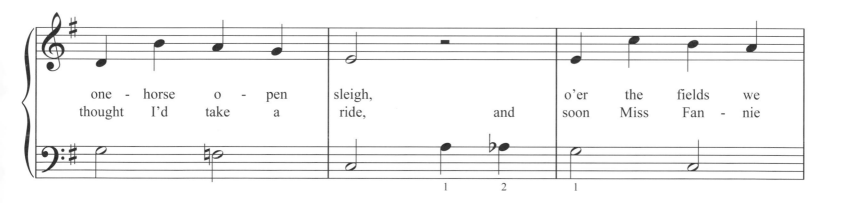

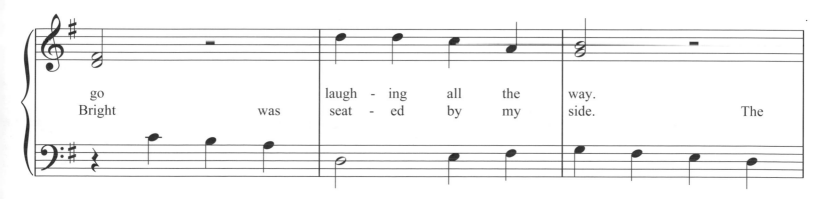

42

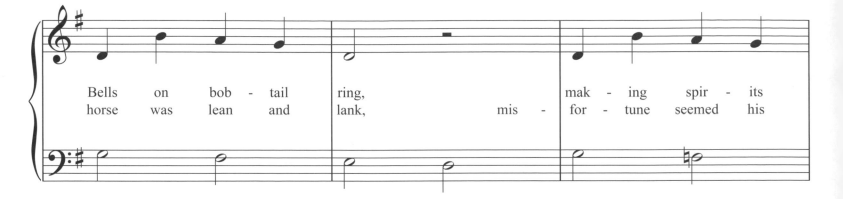

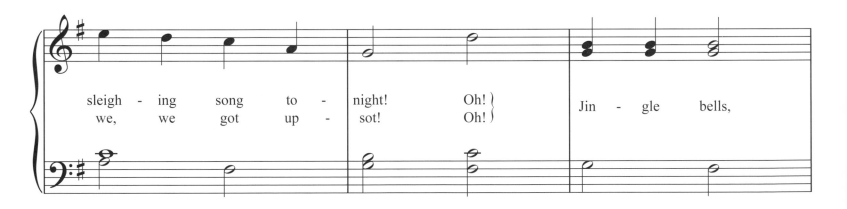

is to ride in a one-horse o-pen sleigh! _____

Jin - gle bells, jin - gle bells, jin - gle all the

way! Oh, what fun it is to ride in a

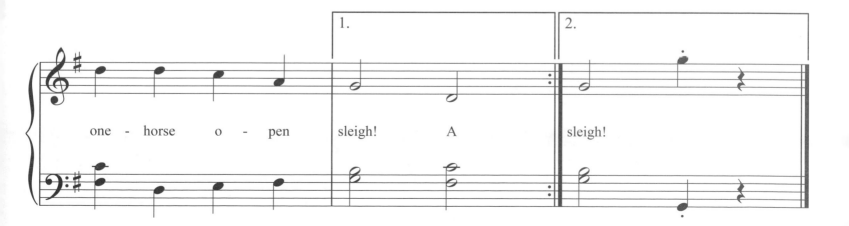

one-horse o-pen sleigh! A sleigh!

I SAW THREE SHIPS

Traditional English Carol

I saw three ships come sail - ing in, on Christ - mas Day, on

Christ - mas Day; I saw three ships come sail - ing in, on

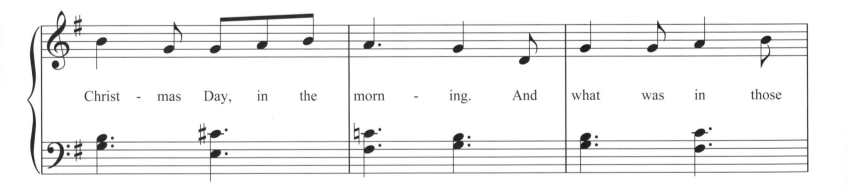

Christ - mas Day, in the morn - ing. And what was in those

ships all three on Christ - mas Day, on Christ - mas Day? And

what was in those ships all three, on Christ-mas Day, in the

morn - ing? The Vir - gin Mar - y and Christ were there, on

Christ - mas Day, on Christ - mas Day; the Vir - gin Mar - y and

Christ were there, on Christ - mas Day in the morn - ing.

IN THE BLEAK MIDWINTER

Poem by CHRISTINA ROSSETTI
Music by GUSTAV HOLST

In the bleak mid - win - ter
What _____ can I give Him,

frost - y wind made moan,
poor _____ as I am?

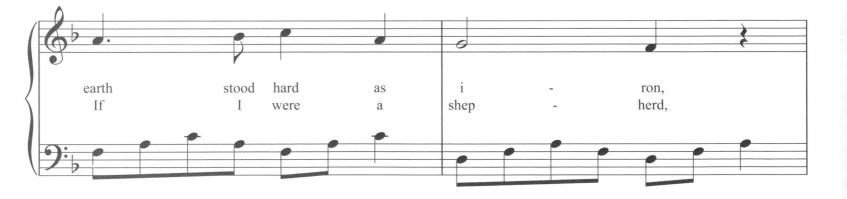

earth stood hard as i - ron,
If I were a shep - herd,

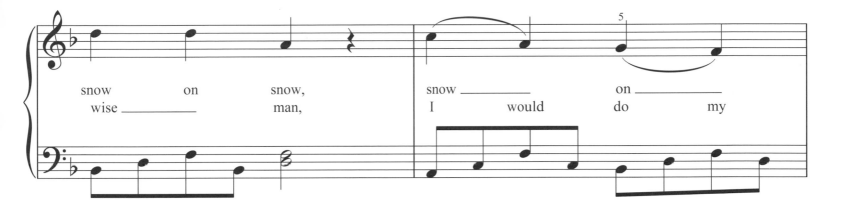

INFANT HOLY, INFANT LOWLY

Traditional Polish Carol
Paraphrased by EDITH M.G. REED

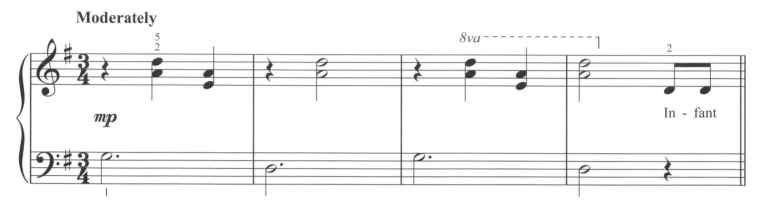

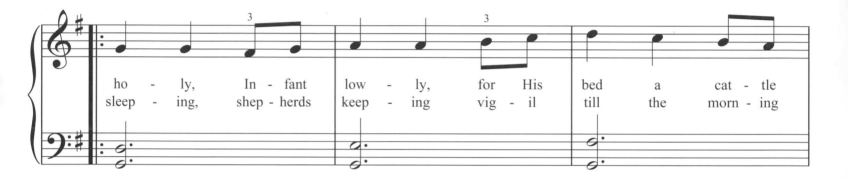

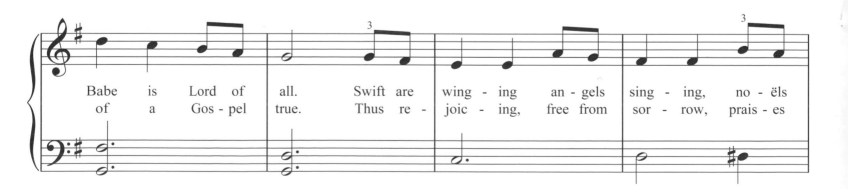

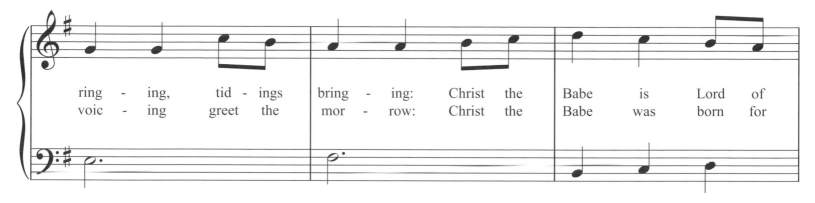

ring - ing, tid - ings bring - ing: Christ the Babe is Lord of
voic - ing greet the mor - row: Christ the Babe was born for

1.

all!

8va

2.

Flocks are you.

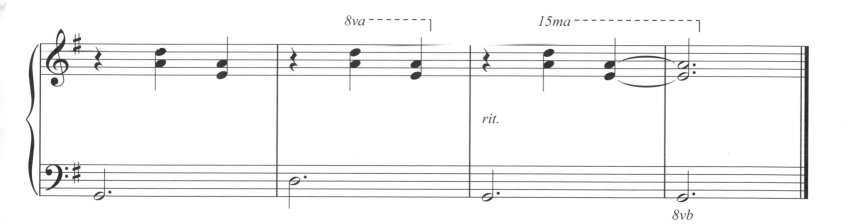

8va   15ma

rit.

8vb

IT CAME UPON THE MIDNIGHT CLEAR

Words by EDMUND HAMILTON SEARS
Music by RICHARD STORRS WILLIS

It came up - on ___ the mid - night

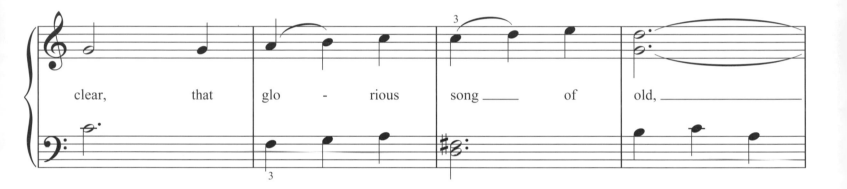

clear, that glo - rious song ___ of old, ___

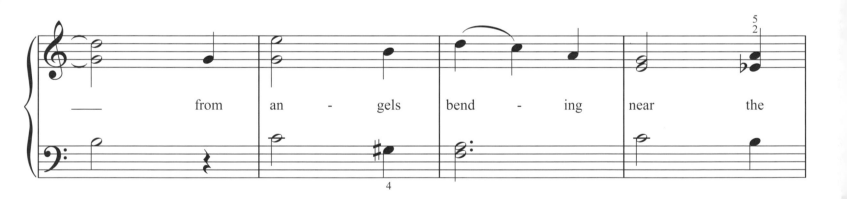

___ from an - gels bend - ing near the

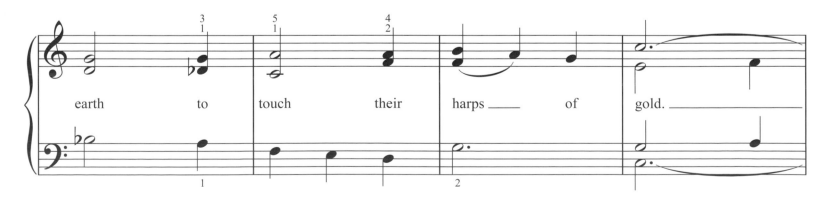

earth to touch their harps ___ of gold. ___

Peace on the earth ___ good - will to

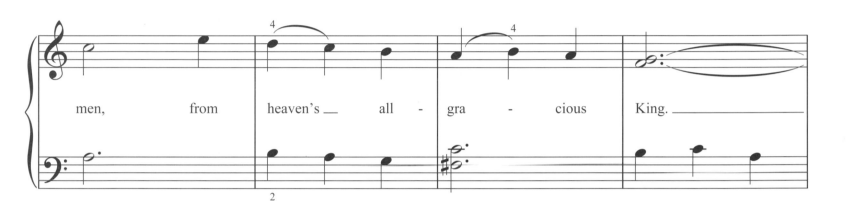

men, from heaven's ___ all - gra - cious King. ___

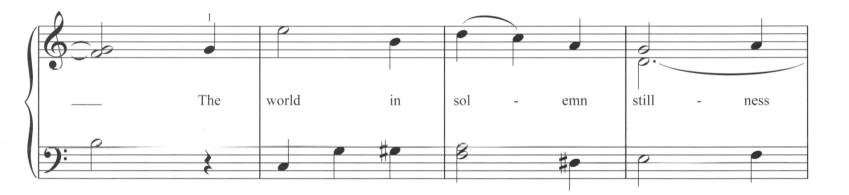

___ The world in sol - emn still - ness

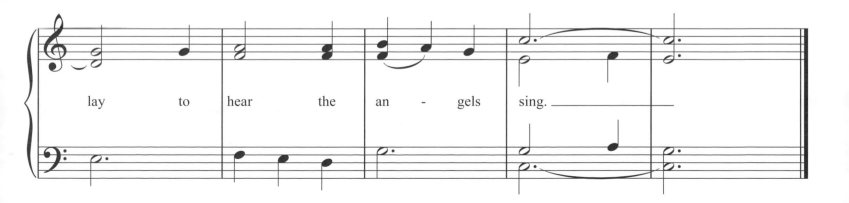

lay to hear the an - gels sing. ___

JOLLY OLD ST. NICHOLAS

Traditional 19th Century American Carol

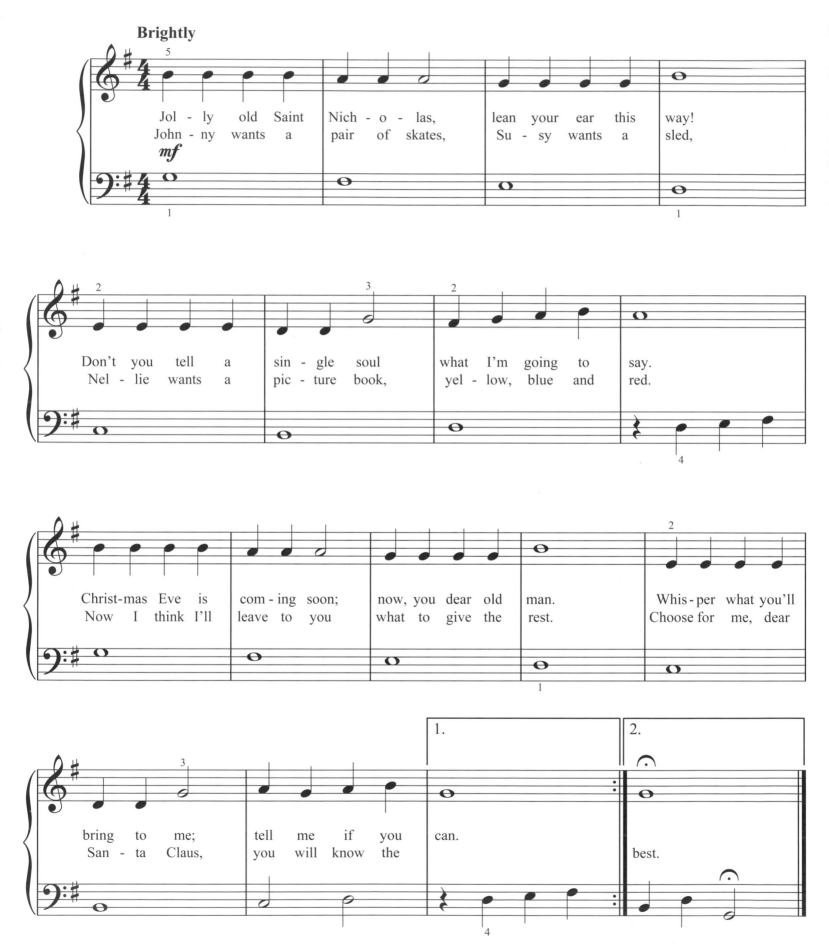

O CHRISTMAS TREE

Traditional German Carol

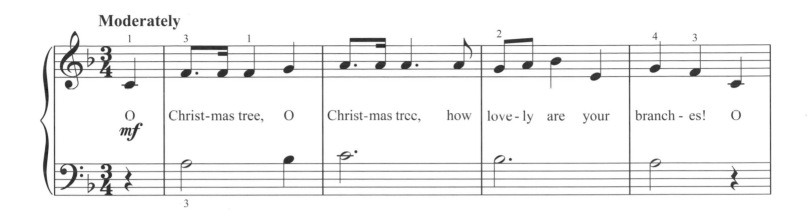

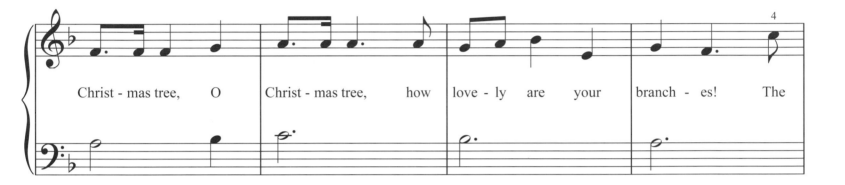

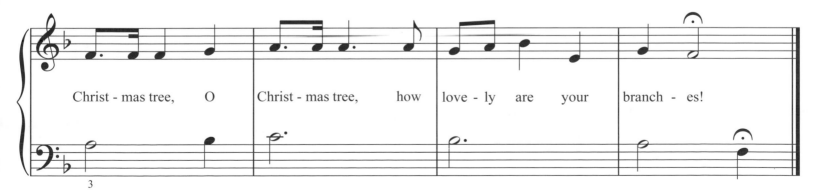

JOY TO THE WORLD

Words by ISAAC WATTS
Music by GEORGE FRIDERIC HANDEL
Adapted by LOWELL MASON

Majestically

Joy to the world, the
He rules the the world

Lord is and come! Let earth re -
truth and grace, and makes the

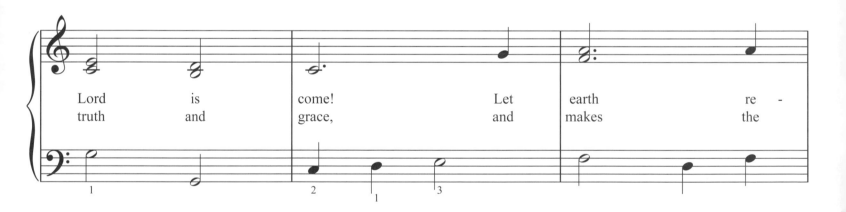

ceive her King. Let ev - 'ry _____
na - tions prove the glo - ries _____

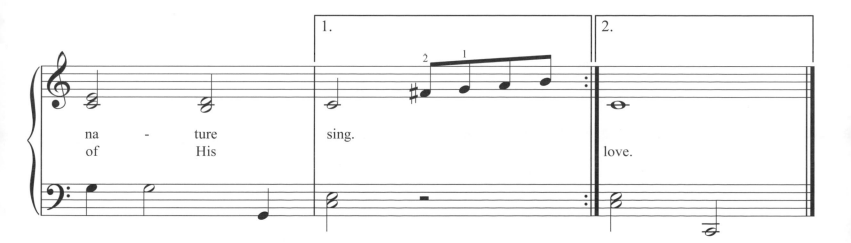

LO, HOW A ROSE E'ER BLOOMING

15th Century German Carol
Translated by THEODORE BAKER
Music from *Alte Catholische Geistliche Kirchengesäng*

Reverently

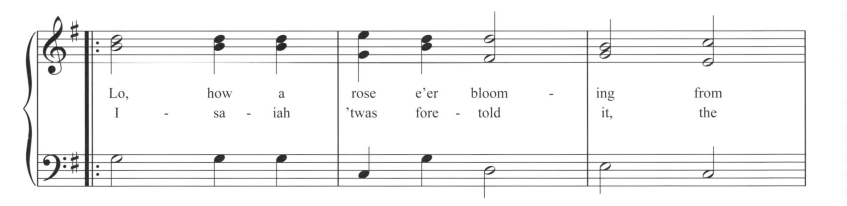

Lo, how a rose e'er bloom - ing, from
I - sa - iah 'twas fore - told it, from the

ten - der stem hath sprung, of Jes - se's
rose I have in mind; with Mar - y

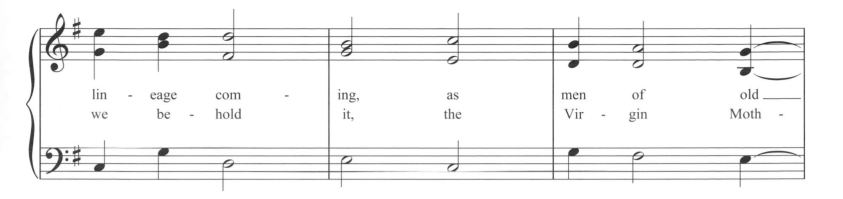

lin - eage com - ing, as the men of old ____
we be - hold it, as the Vir - gin Moth -

___ have sung. It came a flow'r - et bright,
\- er kind. To show God's love a - right

a - mid the cold of win - ter, when
she bore for us a Sav - ior, when

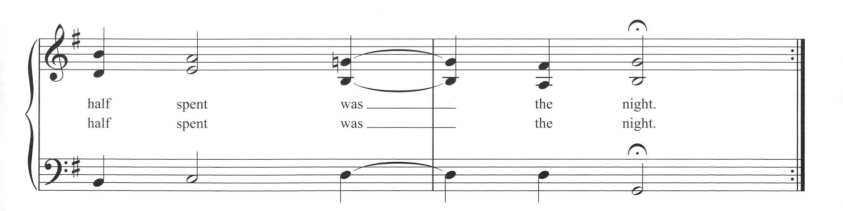

half spent was _____ the night.
half spent was _____ the night.

MASTERS IN THIS HALL

Traditional English

Vigorously

Mas - ters in this hall, _____ hear ye news to - day, _____ brought from o - ver

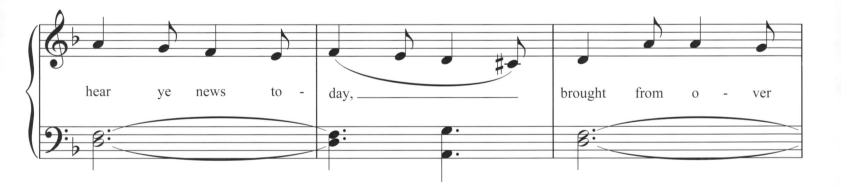

seas, and ev - er I you pray.

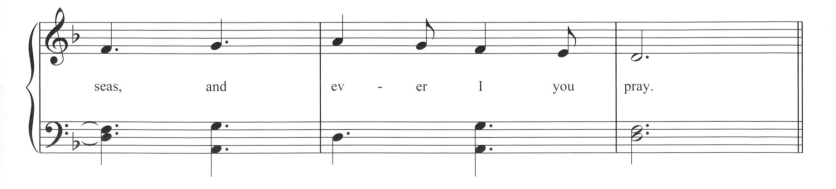

No - ël! No - ël! No - ël! No - ël sing we
No - ël! No - ël! No - ël! No - ël sing we

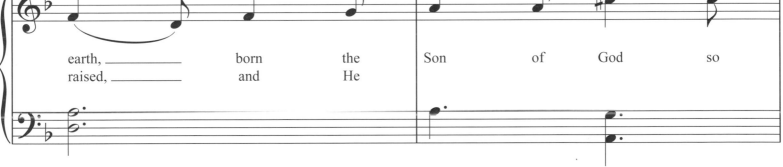

clear! Hol - pen are all folk on
loud! God to - day hath poor folk

1.

earth, _____ born the Son of God so
raised, _____ and He

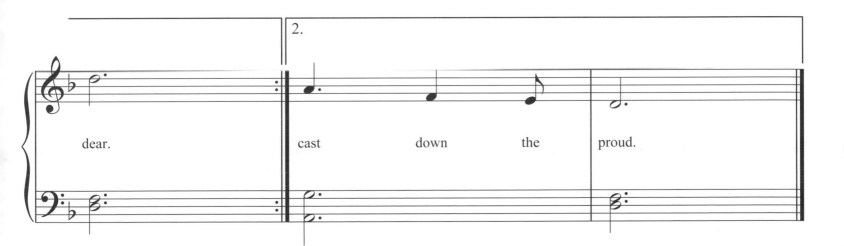

2.

dear. cast down the proud.

O COME, ALL YE FAITHFUL

Music by JOHN FRANCIS WADE
Latin Words translated by FREDERICK OAKELEY

Triumphantly

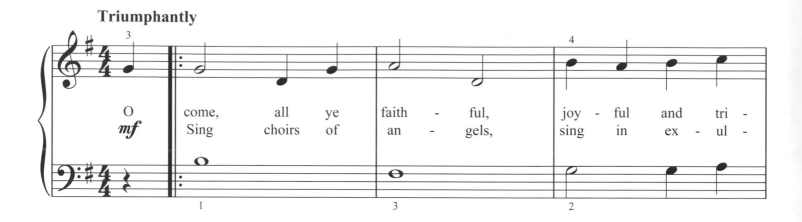

O come, all ye faith - ful,
joy - ful and tri -
mf Sing all choirs of an - gels,
sing in ex - ul -

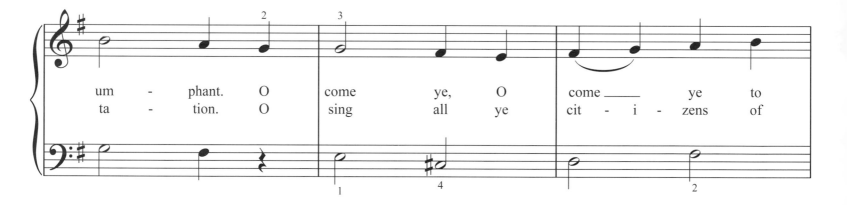

um - phant. O come ye, O
come _____ ye to
ta - tion. O come sing ye all ye
cit - i - zens of

Beth - le - hem.
Come and be -
heav - en a - bove.
Glo - ry to

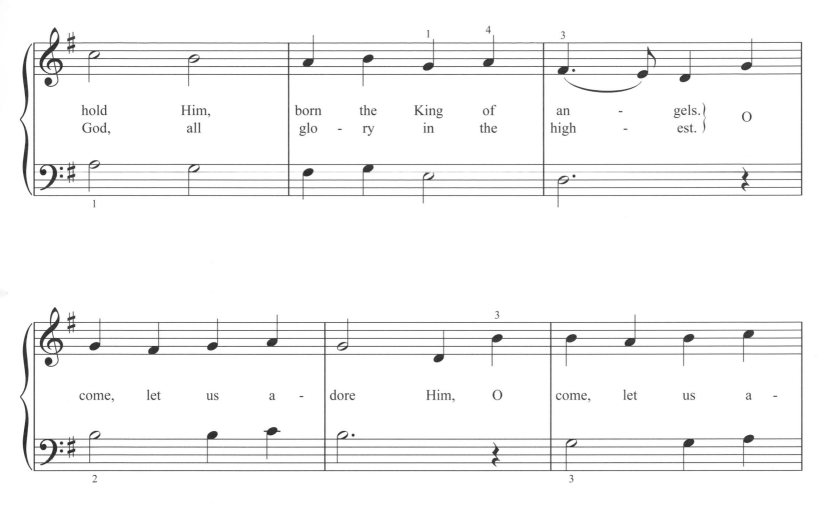

hold Him, born the King of an - gels.}
God, all glo - ry in the high - est. } O

come, let us a - dore Him, O come, let us a -

dore Him, O come, let us a - dore Him, _____

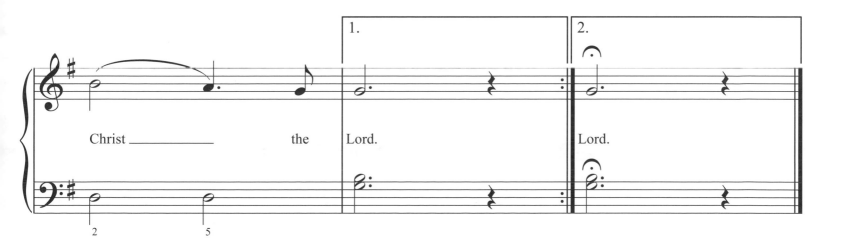

Christ _____ the Lord.

1.
2.
Lord.

O COME, O COME IMMANUEL

Plainsong, 13th Century
Words translated by JOHN M. NEALE
and HENRY S. COFFIN

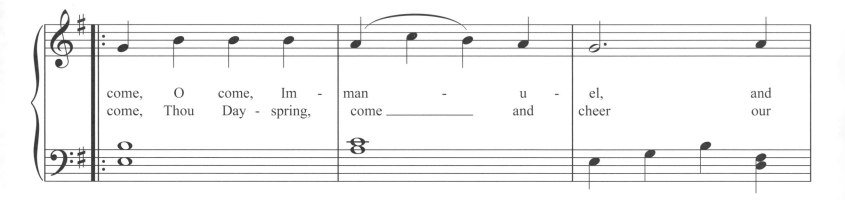

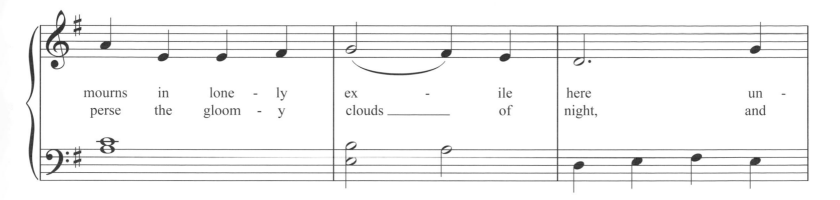

mourns in lone - ly ex - ile here un -
perse the gloom - y clouds _____ of night, and

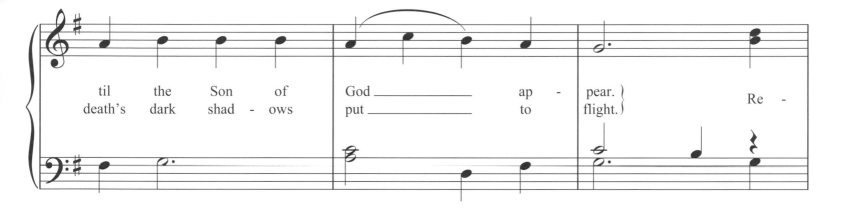

til the Son of God _____ ap - pear.
death's dark shad - ows put _____ to flight. Re -

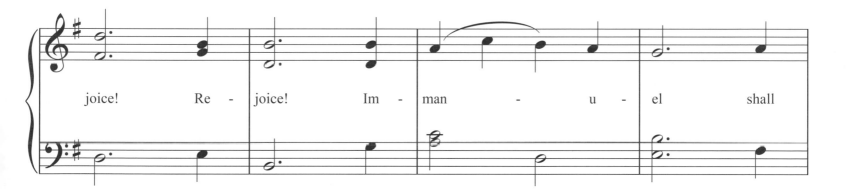

joice! Re - joice! Im - man - u - el shall

come to thee, O Is - ra - el! O el!

O HOLY NIGHT

French Words by PLACIDE CAPPEAU
English Words by JOHN S. DWIGHT
Music by ADOLPHE ADAM

O ho - ly
Tru - ly He

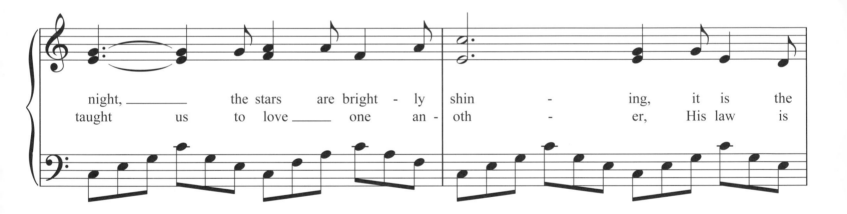

night, _____ the stars are bright - ly shin - ing, it is the
taught us to love _____ one an - oth - er, His law is

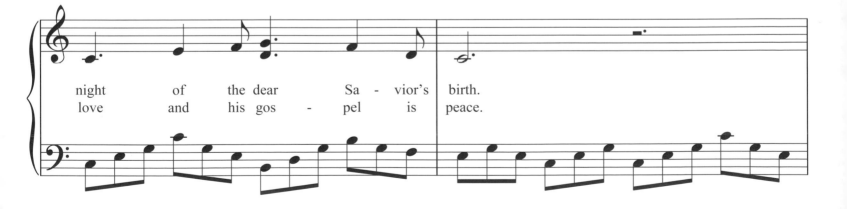

night of the dear Sa - vior's birth.
love and his gos - pel is peace.

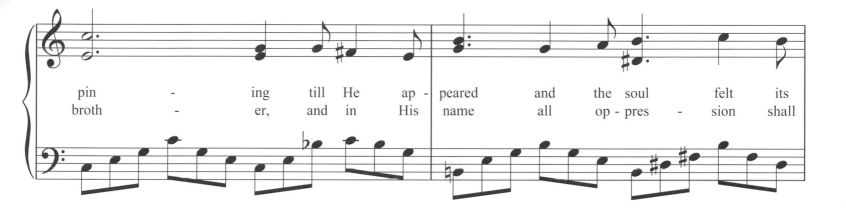

66

new   and glo - rious morn.
praise His ho - ly name.

Fall _____ on your
Christ _____ is the

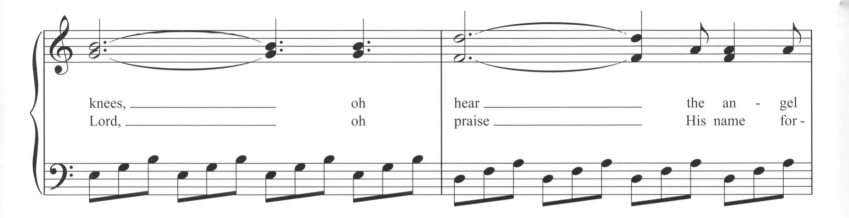

knees, _____ oh
Lord, _____ oh

hear _____ the an - gel
praise _____ His name for -

voic - es.   O
ev - er.   His

night _____ di -
pow'r _____ and

vine, _____ O ___
glo - ry ___ ev -

night _____ when Christ was
er - more pro -

born. _____ O
claim. _____ His

night, _____ O
pow'r _____ and

1.

ho - ly night, O night di -

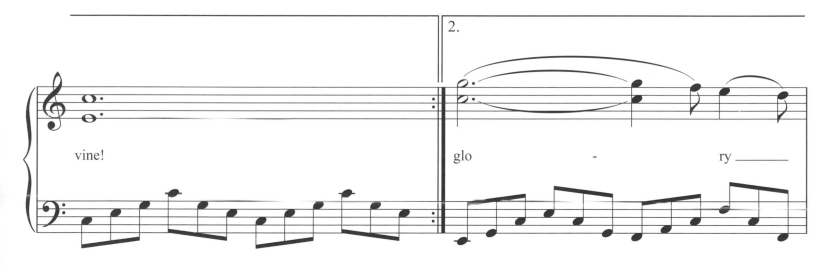

2.

vine! glo - ry _____

ev - er - more pro - claim.

rit.

O LITTLE TOWN OF BETHLEHEM

Words by PHILLIPS BROOKS
Music by LEWIS H. REDNER

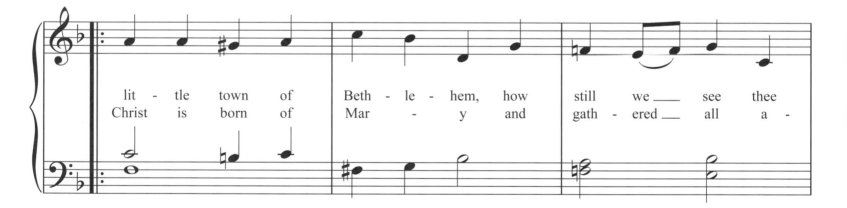

lit - tle town of Beth - le - hem, how still we ___ see thee
Christ is born of Mar - y and gath - ered ___ all a -

lie! A - bove thy deep and dream - less sleep the
bove, while mor - tals deep sleep, and the an - gels keep their

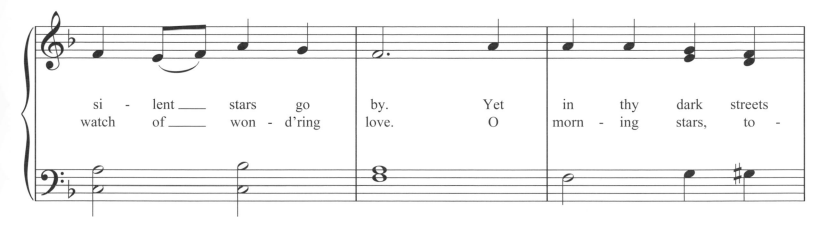

si - lent ___ stars go by. Yet in thy dark streets
watch of ___ won - d'ring love. O morn - ing stars, to -

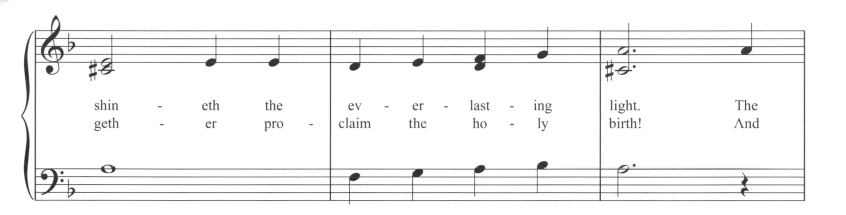

shin - eth the ev - er - last - ing light. The
geth - er pro - claim the ho - ly birth! And

hopes and fears of all the years are met in thee to -
prais - es sing to God the King, and peace to all on

1.
night. For
2.
earth!

OF THE FATHER'S LOVE BEGOTTEN

Words by AURELIUS C. PRUDENTIUS
Translated by JOHN M. NEALE
and HENRY W. BAKER
13th Century Plainsong
Arranged by C. Winfred Douglas

Gently flowing

Of the Fa-ther's love be-
O ye heights of heav'n, a-

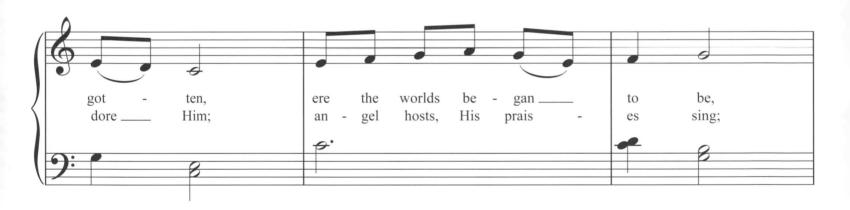

got - ten,   ere the worlds be-gan ___ to   be,
dore ___ Him;   an-gel hosts, His prais- es   sing;

He   is   Al-pha   and   O-me-ga,   He   the Source, the End-
pow'rs, do-min-ions, bow be-fore ___ Him   and ex-tol our God ___

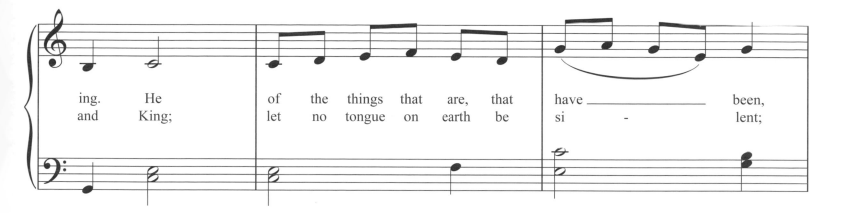

ing.   He   of   the things that are, that   have _____ been,
and   King;   let   no tongue on earth be   si - lent;

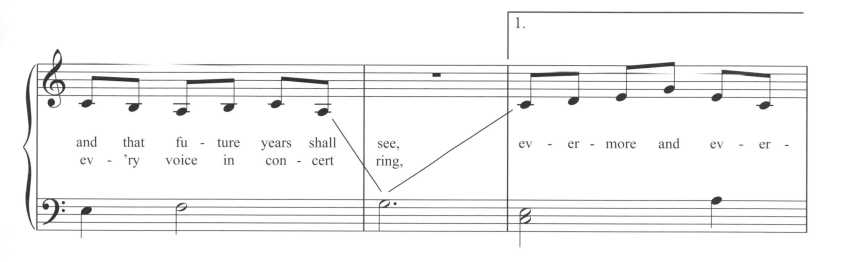

1.

and   that fu - ture years shall   see,   ev - er - more and ev - er -
ev - 'ry voice in con - cert   ring,

2.

more. _____   ev - er - more and ev - er - more. _____

ONCE IN ROYAL DAVID'S CITY

Words by CECIL F. ALEXANDER
Music by HENRY J. GAUNTLETT

Gently

Once in roy - al
And our eyes at

Da - vid's cit - y   stood a low - ly cat - tle __ shed,   where a moth - er
last __ shall __ see Him, through His own re - deem - ing __ love,   for that Child so

laid __ her __ ba - by   in a man - ger   for __ His __ bed.
dear __ and __ gen - tle   is our Lord   in   heav'n __ a - bove.

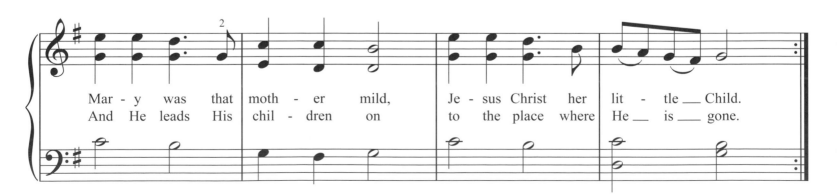

Mar - y was that moth - er mild,   Je - sus Christ her   lit - tle __ Child.
And He leads His chil - dren on   to the place where   He __ is __ gone.

SING WE NOW OF CHRISTMAS

Traditional French Carol

Joyfully, in 2

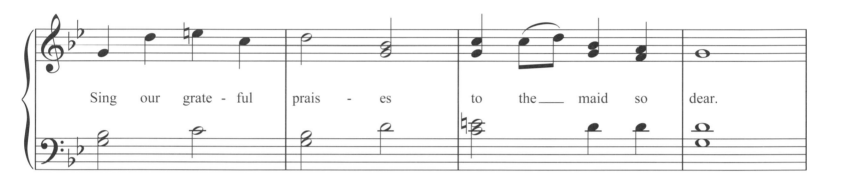

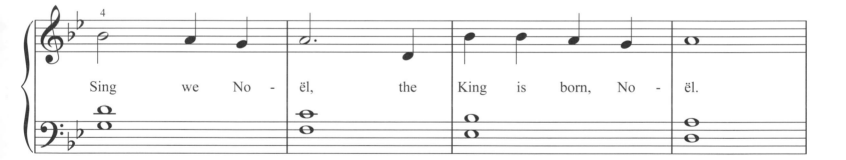

PAT-A-PAN
(Willie, Take Your Little Drum)

Words and Music by
BERNARD de la MONNOYE

March tempo

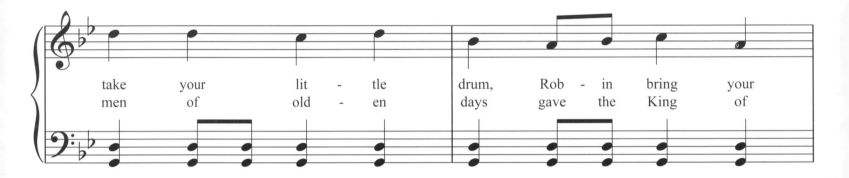

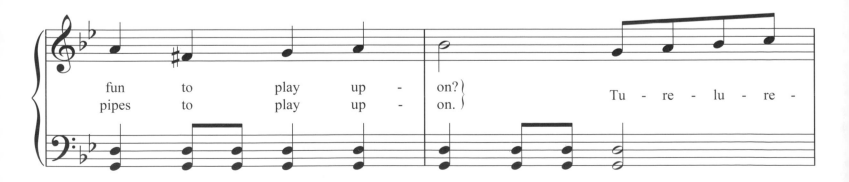

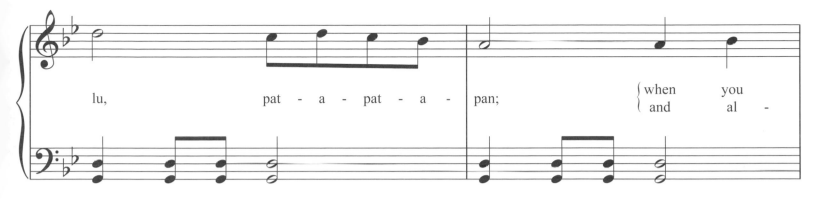

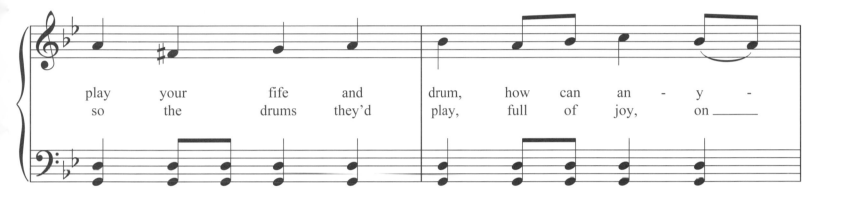

SILENT NIGHT

Words by JOSEPH MOHR
Translated by JOHN F. YOUNG
Music by FRANZ X. GRUBER

Gently

Si - lent night, ho - ly
Si - lent night, ho - ly

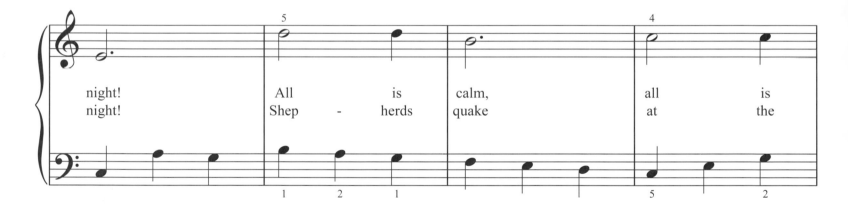

night! All is calm, all is
night! Shep - herds quake at the

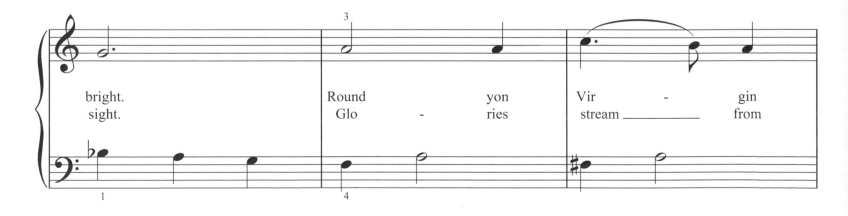

bright. Round yon Vir - gin
sight. Glo - ries stream _____ from

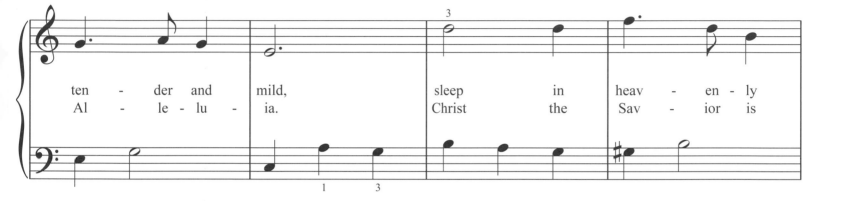

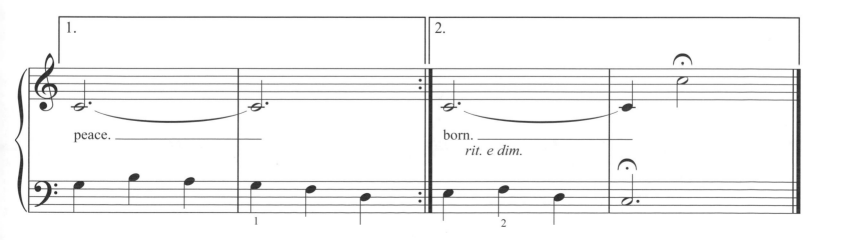

SUSSEX CAROL

Traditional English Carol

On Christ - mas night all Chris - tians sing, to

hear the news ___ the an - gels bring. On Christ - mas night all

our the Re - deem - er made us glad? On Then why should men all on

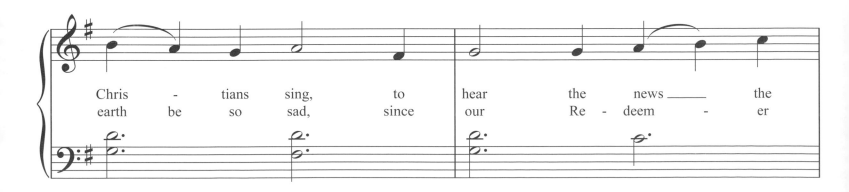

Chris - tians sing, to hear the news ___ the

earth be so sad, since our Re - deem - er

an - gels bring. News of great joy,___ news of ___ great
made us glad? When of from our sin ___ He set ___ us

mirth, news of our
free, all for to

mer - ci - ful ___ King's birth. ___
gain our lib - er - ty. ___

1.

2.

Then

TOMORROW SHALL BE
MY DANCING DAY

Traditional

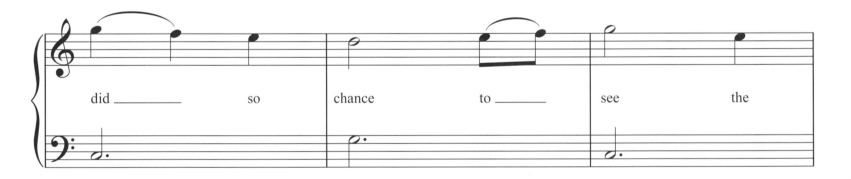

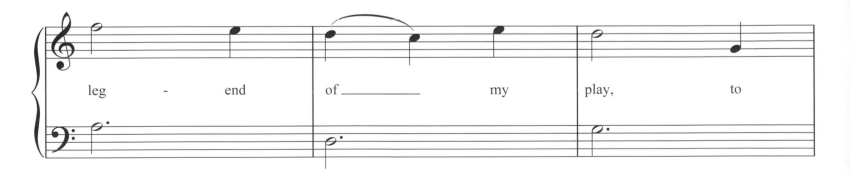

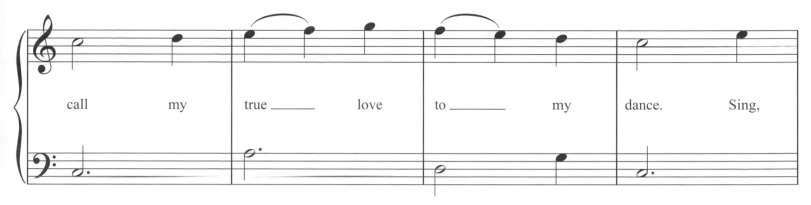

call my true _____ love to _____ my dance. Sing,

O my _____ love, O _____ my

love, my love, my love. This have I

done _____ for my _____ true love. _____

THE TWELVE DAYS OF CHRISTMAS

Traditional English Carol

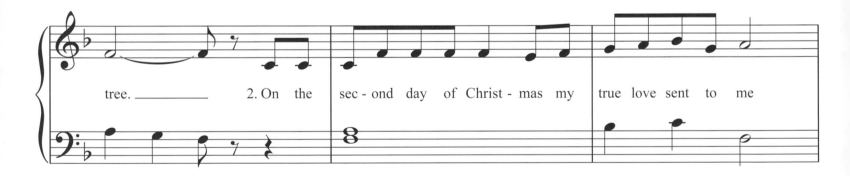

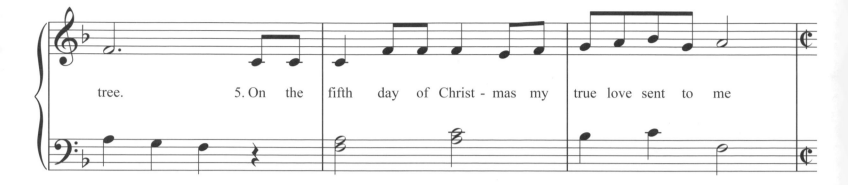

tree.　　5. On the fifth day of Christ - mas my true love sent to me

Slow and broad　　　　　　　　　　　　　　　　　　**Tempo Primo**

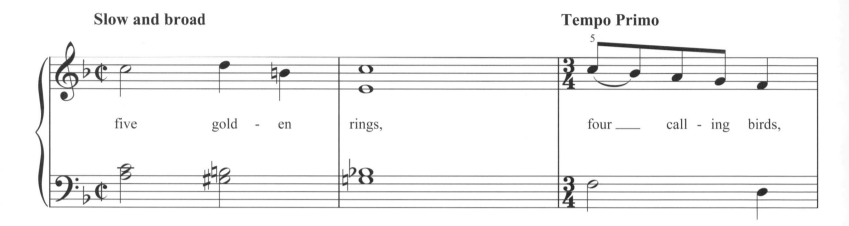

five　gold - en rings,　　　four ___ call - ing birds,

three French hens,　two ___ tur - tle doves and a par - tridge ___ in a pear

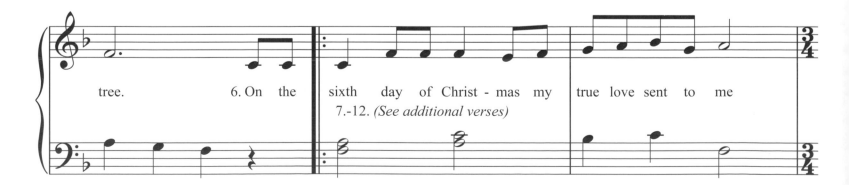

tree.　　6. On the sixth day of Christ - mas my true love sent to me

7.-12. (See additional verses)

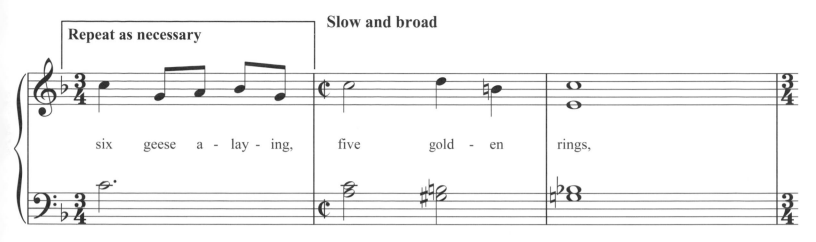

Slow and broad

Repeat as necessary

six geese a-lay-ing, five gold-en rings,

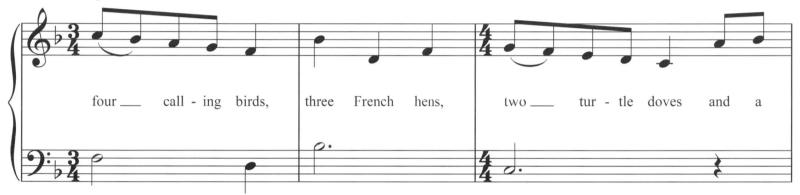

Tempo Primo

four ___ call-ing birds, three French hens, two ___ tur-tle doves and a

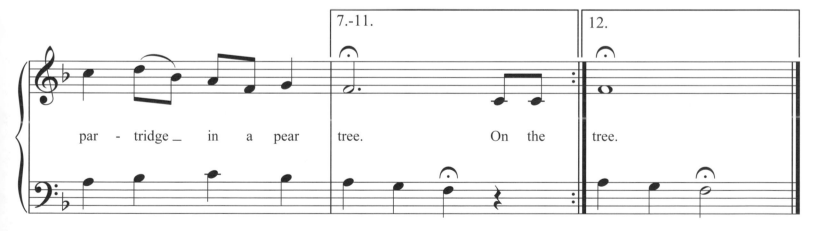

7.-11.

12.

par-tridge ___ in a pear tree. On the tree.

Additional Verses

Seven swans a-swimming
Eight maids a-milking
Nine ladies dancing
Ten lords a-leaping
Eleven pipers piping
Twelve drummers drumming

WE THREE KINGS OF ORIENT ARE

Words and Music by
JOHN H. HOPKINS, JR.

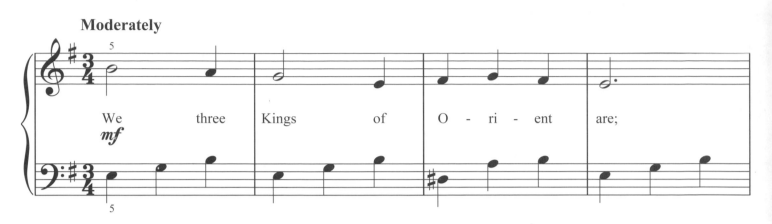

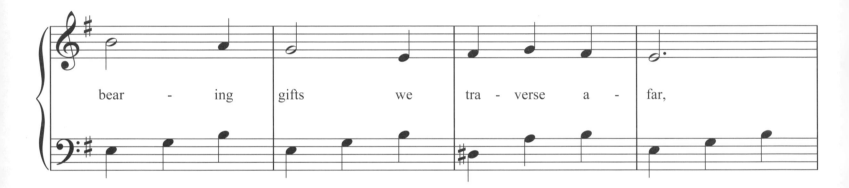

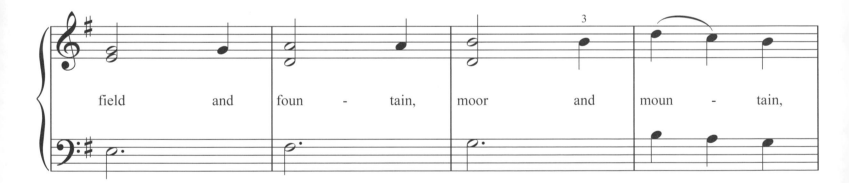

star   of   won - der,   star   of   night,

star   with   roy - al   beau - ty   bright,

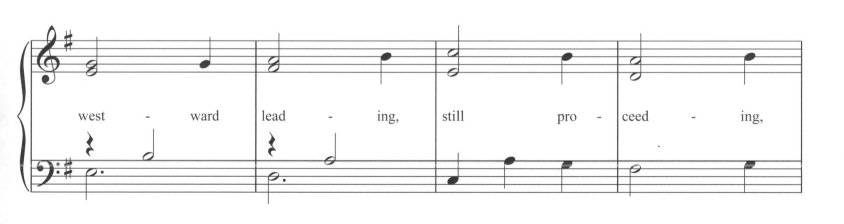

west - ward   lead - ing,   still   pro - ceed - ing,

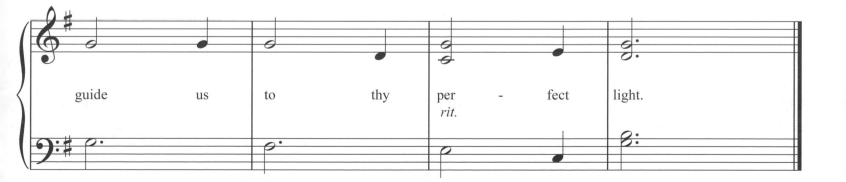

guide   us   to   thy   per - fect   light.

rit.

WE WISH YOU A MERRY CHRISTMAS

Traditional English Folksong

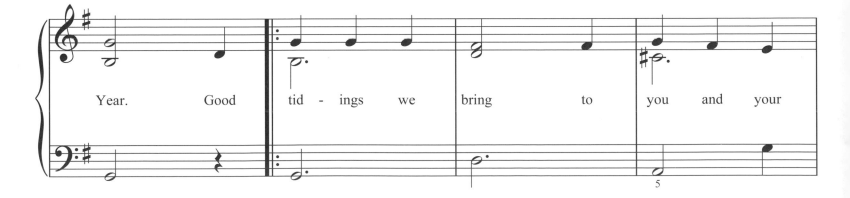

WEXFORD CAROL

Traditional Irish Carol

Moderately

Good peo - ple __ all, this Christ - mas time, con -
night be - fore that hap - py tide, the

sid - er well __ and bear in mind, what our good __ God for
no - ble Vir - gin and her guide were long - time __ seek - ing

us has done in send - ing His __ be - lov - ed Son. With
up and down to find a lodg - ing in the town. But

Mar - y ho - ly we should pray to
mark how all things came to pass, from

God with love ___ this Christ - mas Day. In
ev - 'ry door ___ re - pell'd, a - las. As

Beth - le - hem, up - on that morn, there
long fore - told, their re - fuge all, was

1.
was a bless - ed Mes - si - ah born. The
but a hum - ble

2.
ox - 's stall.

WHAT CHILD IS THIS?

Words by WILLIAM C. DIX
16th Century English Melody

Slowly

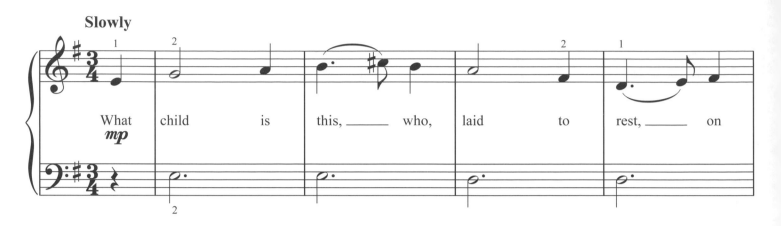

What child is this, _____ who, laid to rest, _____ on

Mar - y's lap _____ is sleep - ing? Whom

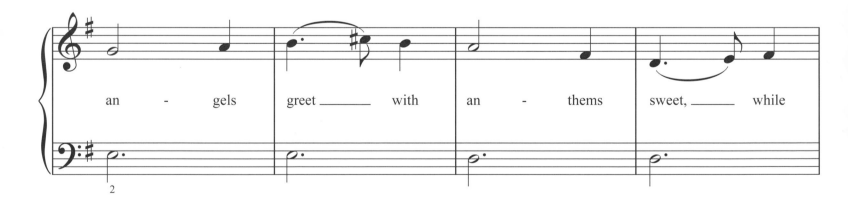

an - gels greet _____ with an - thems sweet, _____ while

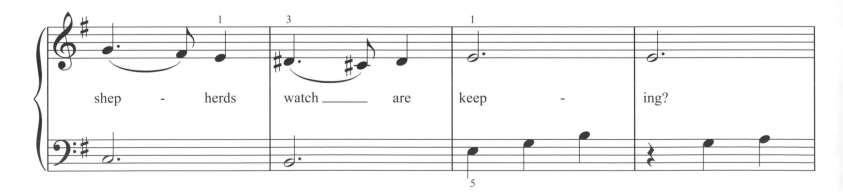

shep - herds watch _____ are keep - ing?

UKRAINIAN BELL CAROL

Traditional
Music by MYKOLA LEONTOVYCH

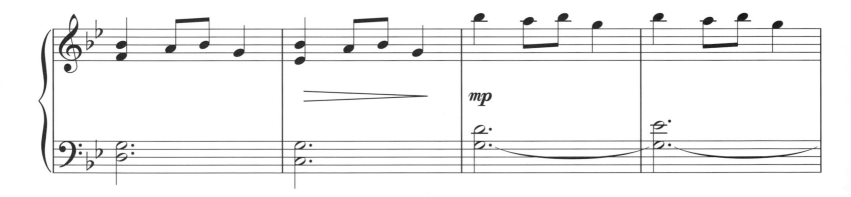

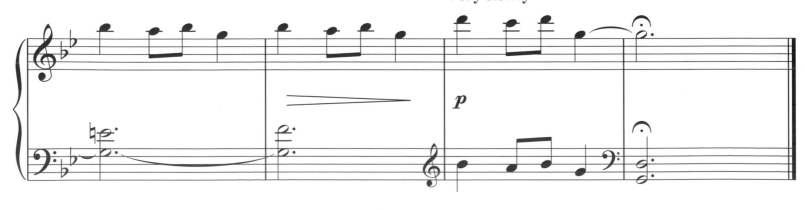